Welcome to China

By Patrick Ryan

The Child's World®

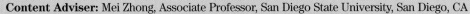

Published by The Child's World®
1980 Lookout Drive
Mankato, MN 56003-1705
800-599-READ
www.childsworld.com

Content Adviser: Mei Zhong, Associate Professor, San Diego State University, San Diego, CA
Design and Production: The Creative Spark, San Juan Capistrano, CA
Editorial: Publisher's Diner, Wendy Mead, Greenwich, CT
Photo Research: Deborah Goodsite, Califon, NJ

Cover and title page: Steve Vidler/SuperStock
Interior photos: Alamy: 16 (Dennis Cox), 19 (Russell Gordon/Danita Delimont), 21 (talissman), 25
(Kevin Foy); Art Resource, NY: 10 (HIP); Corbis: 6 (Craig Lovell), 7 (Keren Su), 12 (Corbis), 15
(Redlink), 18 (Adrian Bradshaw/epa), 23 (Michael S. Yamashita); Getty Images: 3, 27 (Guang Niu);
iStockphoto.com: 3, 9 (Tamir Niv), 11 (Cat London), 28 (Ufuk Zivana), 29 (Jean Schweitzer), 30
(Harry Hu); Mira.com: 13 (Bowater), 20 (Teri L. Gilman); NASA Earth Observatory: 4 (Reto Stockli);
Oxford Scientific: 8 (Tibor Bognar/Photononstop), 3, 26 (Panorama Media (Beijing) Ltd); Panos
Pictures: 17 (Dieter Telemans), 22, 24 (Mark Henley).
Map: XNR Productions: 5

Library of Congress Cataloging-in-Publication Data
Ryan, Patrick, 1948–
  Welcome to China / Patrick Ryan.
     p. cm. — (Welcome to the world)
  Includes index.
  ISBN-13: 978-1-59296-912-8 (library bound : alk. paper)
  ISBN-10: 1-59296-912-7 (library bound : alk. paper)
 1. China—Juvenile literature. I. Title.

DS706.R937 2007
951—dc22
                              2007005553

Contents

Where Is China?

If you could float high above Earth, you would see huge land areas surrounded by water. These land areas are called **continents.** Most of the continents are made up of several countries. China is a huge country on the continent of Asia. China lies next to the Pacific Ocean.

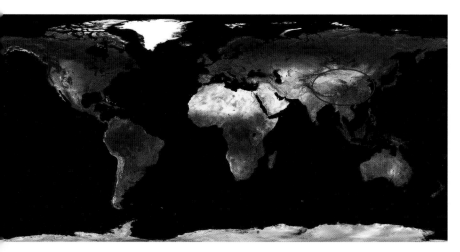

This picture provides a flat view of Earth. China is located in and near the red circle.

The Land

Since China is so big, there are many different land areas. Some areas are called **plateaus.** A plateau is a flat area that is higher than the other areas of land around it. The Inner Mongolian Plateau is an area in China that has bitterly cold winters and very hot summers. The Tibetan Plateau is

In the distance you can see one of the many mountains that surround the Tibetan Plateau.

surrounded by rough, jagged mountains. Besides the plateaus, there are three other important areas in China. The North China Plain is a flat area that is surrounded by mountains on three sides. Central China has lots of people and huge cities. Southern China is covered with rice fields.

A young woman harvests rice from a field in Longji.

A panda snacks on some bamboo.

Plants and Animals

China has many different kinds of plants and animals. In fact, it is home to some of the world's most interesting creatures. One of the best-known animals in China is the panda. It lives in the bamboo forests of southwestern China. Pandas eat bamboo plants that grow in the forests.

Yaks are wild cows that live in the snowy mountain areas of China. They have long, shaggy hair that covers their bodies. This hair keeps them warm and dry. The yaks travel high in the mountains on dangerous paths.

From far away, the big yaks look like boats on a white sea! That's why many people call them "ships of the plateau."

Yaks have thick fur that protects them from the cold.

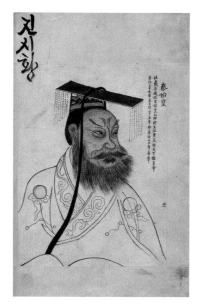

Qin Shihuang was the first emperor of China.

Long Ago

China is a very old country. Until recently, it was ruled by kings called **emperors**. Emperors were born into families of rulers. These royal families were called **dynasties**. China may have been named for the Qin (ch-in) dynasty.

The first emperor, Qin Shihuang, belonged to the Qin dynasty. Long ago, Qin Shihuang built a wall across northern China to keep out his enemies. This wall was almost 6,000 miles (9,656 kilometers) long! Today, we call it the Great Wall. Almost half of it is still standing.

Did you know?

The Great Wall of China is the only human-made object that can be seen from outer space.

China Today

China's last emperor was a six-year-old boy named Pu Yi. Many people disagreed with the way Pu Yi was ruling the country. In 1912, he and his government were overthrown by Dr. Sun Yat-sen and the Nationalist Republican Army.

When people overthrow their rulers, it's called a **revolution**.

In 1949, a new government formed under a man named Mao Zedong (ma-oh say-dong). This government believed in an idea called **communism**.

Mao Zedong talks to schoolchildren after the revolution.

Governments that practice communism believe that property should belong to the whole country instead of individual people. China is one of the few countries that still practices communism today.

Did you **know?**

China has existed for a long time. More than 3,000 years ago, Chinese people were already living in towns. They had even invented a way to write!

Portraits of Mao Zedong can be found in many parts of the country.

The People

China has the most people of any country in the world—more than one billion. That's four times more than the number of people in the United States. With so many people, the biggest problem in China is making sure that everyone has enough to eat. All of China's people need food, but there just isn't enough for everyone. To keep the population from growing too much, the government has said that families should have only one child.

Did you know?

There are 56 different ethnic, or cultural, groups living in China. Most people are members of the Han people.

A busy shopping area in Guangzhou

Bicycles are a popular way to get around in China's cities.

City Life and Country Life

More than 200 million people live in China's cities. Some city people live in large apartment buildings. Others live in small houses with tile roofs. China's cities are so crowded that it's often easier to travel by bicycle instead of by car. Many people also travel on trains.

Country life in China is very different from city life. Many country people live in houses with only a few rooms—a kitchen, a bedroom, and sometimes a bathroom. Most of them work as

A girl tends to her sheep in the Shaanxi province.

farmers. Other families live on small cargo boats called **sampans**. People who live on sampans carry goods up and down the rivers. In the mountain areas of China, some country people live in caves.

17

Schools and Language

Chinese children start school when they are seven years old. They begin each day with thirty minutes of exercise! In school, Chinese students learn to write when they are very young. They also learn how to do math by

A student practices writing.

moving beads on an **abacus**. An abacus is a very old tool for counting.

Almost everyone in China speaks Chinese, but they don't all speak it the same way. That means that a Chinese speaker from one area might not be able to understand the Chinese spoken in another area. Mandarin Chinese is the official dialect, or type, of China. Mandarin is mostly spoken in the north. People in the south speak many different kinds of Chinese, including Cantonese.

These elementary students are studying Chinese and social studies.

A farmer plows his field with help from his ox.

Work

More than half of all Chinese people are farmers. They grow rice, wheat, grains, and other crops like cotton and tea. They also raise pigs and chickens. Many Chinese farmers still do all their work by hand or with a plow pulled by an animal.

These factory workers are making appliances.

China is growing and changing every day. Today, millions of people work in factories instead of farming. They make televisions, radios, video games, and even cars! They also make clothes, shoes, sports equipment, and toys. The things China makes are sold all over the world.

21

Food

There are many different styles of food in China depending on where you go. In the Southeast, you might find shark fin or bird's nest soup. Spicy dishes are popular in the Hunan and Sichuan areas of western China. And, across the country, many Chinese people like to eat pork, beef, chicken, and vegetables, just like you.

The Chinese serve many foods with rice or noodles. And instead of using forks, people eat with special sticks called **chopsticks**.

A boy eats noodles at a local food market.

22

Chopsticks are used by either scooping or pinching food to lift it up to a person's mouth. Chinese people also have their favorite drink with most meals—tea! China grows some of the best tea in the world.

Did you know?

In China, children like to snack on fruit, crackers, candy, and even American-style fast food.

These children are studying martial arts at a school in the Henan province.

Pastimes

People in China enjoy music, plays, movies, and sports. Ping pong, swimming, volleyball, gymnastics, and soccer are all favorite sports. Another favorite table game is called *mah-jongg*. It's similar to the card game called rummy. But it's played with small tiles instead of cards.

Every morning, millions of people exercise by performing **t'ai chi chuan** (ty chee chon) in parks and courtyards. Tai chi chuan is an ancient form of exercise that has 128 different movements. The

A group of kids play soccer in the park.

movements are slow and graceful. Many people also like to do forms of self-defense called wu shu, or **martial arts**.

Lots of people attend the Spring Festival.

Holidays

The Chinese people love holidays. The biggest celebration in China is the Spring Festival. Another name for this holiday is the Chinese New Year. It's celebrated in January or February. The actual date of the Chinese New Year depends on where the moon is in the sky. This date changes every year.

A young girl performs at the Spring Festival.

China is an interesting place. It's home to many different kinds of plants and animals. There are hundreds of old buildings to visit. And China has some of the most beautiful countryside in the world. The Chinese people are polite to strangers and they welcome visitors from other countries. So if you ever go to China, be sure to smile—China will smile back!

27

Fast Facts About China

Area: 3,705,000 square miles (9,596,960 square kilometers)—a little larger than the United States.

Population: Over 1.3 billion people.

Capital City: Beijing.

Other Important Cities: Shanghai, Tianjin, Chongqing, Guangzhou.

Money: The yuan. One yuan is divided into 10 jiao.

Important Holiday: Spring Festival. It is also known as the Chinese New Year. This holiday happens in late January or early February.

Highest mountain: Mount Everest. It is 29,035 feet (8,850 meters) high. Mount Everest is the highest mountain in the world.

National Flag: A red flag with five yellow stars. The four smaller stars represent the people of China. The big star represents China's government. The red color represents the revolution that created modern China.

National Song:

"March of the Volunteers"
    Arise,
    Ye who refuse to be slaves!
    With our very flesh and blood,
    Let us build our new Great Wall!
    The peoples of China are in the most
        critical time,
    Everybody must roar his defiance.
    Arise!
    Arise!
    Arise!
    Millions of hearts with one mind,
    Brave the enemy's gunfire, march on!
    Brave the enemy's gunfire, march on!
    March on!
    March on!
    On!

Famous People:

Confucius: great educator, philosopher

Lu Chen: Olympic figure skater

Qin Shihuang: founder of the first Chinese Empire

Deng Xiaoping: political leader, economic reformer

Mao Zedong: founder of the People's Republic of China

Chinese Folklore:

The First Emperor's Tomb

Qin Shihuang, China's first emperor, was buried near Mount Li. His tomb was the size of a small city and it took more than 30 years to build. Along with the buildings, the emperor had thousands of clay sculptures made to look like all kinds of soldiers. More than 7,000 of these warriors stood guard over the emperor in his tomb.

His tomb remained hidden for centuries until farmers discovered it by accident in the 1970s. It was found buried underground. After the tomb was uncovered, scientists began working on the site. They continue to unearth the tomb and have found thousands of objects so far.

How Do You Say...

ENGLISH	CHINESE	HOW TO SAY IT
hello	ni hao	nee-how
goodbye	zai jian	tzee-jen
please	qing	ching
thank you	xiexie	shyeh-shyeh
one	yi	ee
two	er	ahr
three	san	sahn
China	Zhongguo	jawng-gwaw

Glossary

abacus (AB-uh-kuss) An abacus is a very old tool that is used for counting. It works by sliding beads along a groove.

chopsticks (CHOP-stiks) Chopsticks are special sticks that people in China use to eat with. Chopsticks are used by either scooping or pinching food to lift it up to a person's mouth.

communism (KOM-yuh-niz-um) Communism is an idea that some governments use to rule their countries. Governments that practice communism believe that property should belong to the whole country instead of individual people.

continents (KON-tuh-nents) All of the land areas on Earth are divided up into huge sections called continents. Most of the continents are separated by oceans.

dynasties (DY-nuh-steez) A dynasty is a family of rulers. Each one of China's emperors came from a dynasty.

emperors (EM-pur-rurz) Emperors are what the kings of China are called. Today, there are no emperors in China.

martial arts (MAR-shul ARTS) Martial arts are forms of self-defense. There are many forms of martial arts.

plateau (pla-TOH) A plateau is a flat area that is higher than the other areas of land around it. Some areas of China are plateaus.

revolution (rev-uh-LOO-shun) When people overthrow their rulers, it's called a revolution.

sampans (SAM-panz) Sampans are small cargo boats. They are used to carry goods up and down rivers.

t'ai chi chuan (ty chee chwahn) T'ai chi chuan is a series of exercises for good health.

Further Information

Read It

Pluckrose, Henry Arthur. *China*. Danbury, CT: Franklin Watts, 2000.

Riehecky, Janet. *A Ticket to China*. Minneapolis, MN: Carolrhoda Books, 1999.

Simonds, Nina, Leslie Swartz, and the Children's Museum, Boston, MA.: *Moonbeams, Dumplings & Dragons: A Treasury of Chinese Holiday Tales, Activities, & Recipes.* Gulliver Books, 2002.

Look It Up

Visit our Web page for lots of links about China:
http://www.childsworld.com/links

Note to Parents, Teachers, and Librarians: We routinely verify our Web links to make sure they are safe, active sites—so encourage your readers to check them out!

Index